I0489506

Executive Summary

This research analyzes the impact of the U.S. Fed bond-buying program on the economy since 2008 and on inflation in particular. The theoretical basics for understanding the present monetary system are illustrated by introducing the monetary multiplier with its corresponding ratios and parameters. The current scientific consensus is also examined by analyzing the latest publications and papers of acknowledged economists. In addition, statistics on money supply and inflation show that the Quantitative Easing Programs from the Fed have no current impact on inflation, which can be considered as reassuring but also alarming. A dramatic buildup of excess reserves as a byproduct of QE is worrying. The largest concern about the end of QE is how to reduce these excess reserves appropriately. Experiences from the Bank of Japan during their orderly exit from Quantitative Easing provide some strategies and alternatives how the Fed can reduce the enormous amount of reserves. Furthermore, the lessons learned from the BoJ show that the composition of assets the Fed has acquired will for the most part determine their approach to exit. This investigation was created as part of a seminar paper of MBA studies at the FOM University of Applied Sciences Berlin, Germany.

Table of Contents

List of Abbreviations

ABCP	Asset-backed commercial paper
BoJ	Bank of Japan
CPI	consumer price index
edn.	Edition
et al.	et alii / et aliae
Fed	Federal Reserve System
Fig.	Figure
FOMC	Federal Open Market Committee
GDP	Gross domestic product
JGB	Japanese government bond
No.	Number
pp.	Pages
QE	Quantitative easing
Vol.	Volume

List of Figures

List of Tables

1. Introduction

"When the helicopter starts dropping money in a steady stream - or, more generally, when the quantity of money starts unexpectedly to rise more rapidly - it takes time for people to catch on to what is happening."

(Milton Friedman)

Source: Friedman, M. (2009), The Optimum Quantity Of Money, p. 13

The allegorical statement of the helicopter from Milton Friedman, one of the most popular economists of the twentieth century, was picked up by Ben S. Bernanke during a speech he gave in 2002. Ben Shalom Bernanke was chairman of the Federal Reserve of the United States of America from 2006 to 2014. After this speech, in which he referenced Friedman's "helicopter drop" theory that claims deflation is best combated by direct infusion of cash to the people, he received his famous nickname "Helicopter-Ben". His nickname became most famous during the financial crisis that started in 2007, a crisis that was never seen before since the economic catastrophe in the 1930s (Doom, 2012). It started in summer of 2007 by the bursting of the United States housing bubble and reached its top in the collapse of the investment bank Lehman Brothers in September of 2008. In November 2008, just 2 months after the collapse of Lehman Brothers, the inflation rate (CPI) on a monthly basis (November 2008 – October 2008) of the United States was about minus 1.9% (U.S. Department of Labor, 2008). According to the macroeconomic doctrine, negative inflation is called deflation and is linearly connected to the money supply (Amy, W. Grady, 2011, p. 164 - 165). In other words, concerns about a massive economic slowdown with an unpredictable impact on the entire society increased rapidly. At this time, the US Fed was willing to support the market liquidity, the market functioning and the pursuit of their macroeconomic objectives through monetary policy (Bernanke, Ben S., 2008). By using the helicopter allegory, Bernanke now started printing and dropping money into the country. This happened in late November of 2008 by buying mortgage-backed securities. Beside other important steps and reactions of the U.S. Fed to the crisis, like new rules for mortgage lenders, the lowering of the Federal funds rate and the discount rate, the new created interest on excess reserve balances and the amount of required reserves were together with the beginning of buying securities the most disputable steps they have done. Since then a lot of discussions and concerns regarding the impact of the decisions made by the Fed are flared up. The most important concern of economists and scientists are the recent and the prospective impact of the Fed's program on inflation. Coming back to the citation I made on the beginning of this introduction, even seven years after the beginning of the crisis and the economic recovery nowadays, the impact of the Fed's quantitative easing program on inflation over the long run is still not foreseeable. The purpose of this research is to give an overview about the theoretical basics of macroeconomic conditions like the money multiplier and the monetary system in general, the main facts of the economic crisis 2007/2008 and the (potential) impact of the Fed's quantitative easing program on inflation. To be more specific I also try to give a draft of possible exit strategies and its potential impact on the recent economy.

2. The Monetary System and the Money Multiplier

In the following the general conditions of the economic system, we are dealing with, will be explained. Therefore it should be clear what we are talking about. A short definition of money, its functions and types, the definition of money supply and the role of the Central Bank and finally the money supply measures will be described. It should be clear that in the context of this research a technical discussion about the history and development about the meaning of money is not possible and useful. Hence the status quo of our modern money concept will be explained.

According to Mankiw (2013) money is the stock of assets that can be readily used to make transactions. Its functions can be summarized as medium of exchange (we use it to buy stuff), store of value (it transfers purchasing power from the present to the future) and as unit of account (the common unit by which everyone measures prices and values). In this context there are two types and categorizations of money which are generally exist. Fiat money has no intrinsic value and is the money we are using every day as e.g. the paper money to buy things. Commodity money has intrinsic value which depends highly on the conditions of the economic environment. Such money is for instance gold as coins or even cigarettes in Prisoner of War camps. To handle the amount and effect of money in a macroeconomic context two other definitions are important. The money supply is the quantity of money (total amount of monetary assets) available in the economy at a specific time. The monetary policy is the control over the money supply. The monetary policy on the other hand is conducted by a country's central bank. In the context of this research the United States central bank, called Federal Reserve (Fed) is the object of investigation. To control the money supply, the Fed uses open market operations, which include the purchase and sale of government bonds (Michl, Thomas R., 2002, p. 65). The money supply measures are shown in the table below.

Symbol	Assets included
C	Currency, also called **M0**
M1	C + demand deposits, travelers' checks, other checkable deposits
M2	**M1** + small time deposits (under $ 100,000), saving deposits, money market mutual funds, money market deposit accounts
M3	**M2** + large denomination ($ 100,000 or more) time deposits, institutional money market funds, short-term repurchase and other larger liquid assets
MZM	**M2** - small denomination time deposits, plus institutional money market mutual funds (money, zero maturity)

Table 1: Money supply measures, Source: Federal Reserve Bank of St. Louis, Research Division, 2014

The money supply which is denoted by **M** equals currency plus demand (**D,** checking account) deposits:

$$M = C + D = \text{currency} + \text{deposits}$$

Since the money supply includes demand deposits, the banking system plays an important role. A few preliminaries in the following regarding the banks' role in the monetary system. The banking system that can be found in the U.S. and Europe is a fractional-reserve banking system, which means, that we have a system in which banks hold a fraction of their deposits as reserves. These Reserves (**R**) are the portion of deposits that banks have not lent. In summary you can say, that a bank's liabilities include deposits, assets include reserves and outstanding loans. The following balance sheet of a fictional bank visualizes the mentioned premises.

Balance sheet of *a bank*			
Assets		**Liabilities and Owners' Equity**	
Reserves	$200	Deposits	$750
Loans	$500	Debt	$200
Securities	$300	Capital (owners' equity)	$50

Table 2: example of a banks' balance sheet, Source: Mankiw, N. Gregory, 2013

In this example the bank is obligated to hold $200 in Reserves, which means by a total of $1.000 deposits on the right side ($750 + $200 + $50) that the bank has to hold 20% of its deposits as reserves. Another important dimension can be defined. The ratio of reserves to deposits (**rr**) which highly depends on regulations and bank policies.

$$rr = \frac{R}{D} = \frac{\text{reserves}}{\text{total deposits}} = \frac{\$200}{\$1,000} = 0.2$$

Now we can calculate the total money supply by the following formula:

$$M = \frac{1}{rr} \cdot D = \frac{1}{\text{ratio of reserves to deposits}} \cdot \text{total deposits} = \frac{1}{0.2} \cdot \$1,000 = \$5,000$$

As a conclusion we can see, that a fractional-reserve banking system creates money (but not necessarily wealth). This is reasoned by the fact, that the loans of a bank can be used from other banks by credits or savings from customers, until the amount drops to almost zero, caused by the amount of reserves that reduces the deposits every time. In other words bank loans give borrowers some new money and an equal amount of new debt (Mankiw, N. Gregory, 2013). Regarding the capital requirement, a minimum amount of capital that is mandated by regulators is used to ensure that the banks will be able to pay off depositors. It is higher for banks that hold more risky assets. A new definition has to be introduced, the monetary base (**B**), which is controlled by the central bank.

$$B = C + R = currency + reserves$$

The currency-deposit ratio (**cr**) is another dimension and depends on households' preferences.

$$cr = \frac{C}{D} = \frac{currency}{deposits}$$

Now we can use the aforementioned dimensions to solve the money supply:

$$M = C + D = \frac{C + D}{B} \cdot B = m \cdot B$$

where

$$m = \frac{C + D}{B} = \frac{C + D}{C + R} = \frac{\left(\frac{C}{D}\right) + \left(\frac{D}{D}\right)}{\left(\frac{C}{D}\right) + \left(\frac{R}{C}\right)} = \frac{cr + 1}{cr + rr}$$

The new dimension **m** is the money multiplier, which by definition means, that an increase in the money supply results from a one dollar increase in the monetary base. It can be noted, if monetary base changes by **ΔB**, than:

$$\Delta M = m \cdot \Delta B$$

$$if\ rr < 1,\ then\ m > 1$$

If households deposit less of their money, then banks cannot make as many loans, so the banking system will not be able to create much money. This means, an increase in **cr** increases the denominator of **m** proportionally more than the numerator. So **m** falls, causing **M** to fall (Mankiw, N. Gregory, 2013).

The instruments of monetary policy should also be mentioned. The Fed can change the monetary base by using open market operations. To increase the monetary base, the Fed could buy government bonds which are paid with new dollars. They also can change the discount rate which is the interest rate the Fed charges on loans on banks. To increase the base, the Fed could lower the discount rate which would encourage the banks to borrow more reserves. To change the reserve-deposit ratio the Fed can change the reserve requirements or could start paying interest on reserves (Mankiw, N. Gregory, 2013).

Now, the relation between the aforementioned dimensions and inflation should be described. It starts with the so called quantity theory of money which is a simple theory that links the inflation rate to the growth rate of the money supply (Jain, T.R. et al, 2006, pp. 267 - 270).

$$M \cdot V = P \cdot Y$$

The denotation of **V** is velocity and is the rate at which money circulates. In other words it is the number of times the average dollar bill changes hands in a given time period. **P** is the price of output, the gross domestic product (GDP) deflator. **Y** is the quantity of output, the real GDP. This quantity equation is an identity, which means it holds by definition of the variables. The theory assumes that velocity is constant; it concludes that the money growth rate determines the inflation rate (in the long run) and is consistent with cross-country and time-series data (Mankiw, N. Gregory, 2013). The inflation rate π can be defined as:

$$\pi = \frac{\Delta M}{M} - \frac{\Delta Y}{Y} = \frac{\Delta P}{P}$$

Nevertheless it should be mentioned that the concept in general is controversial. A lot of scientists, above all Keynes, argue that a change in the quantity of money has only an indirect effect on price-level (Jain, T.R. et al, 2006, pp. 62 - 81, Ball, R. James, 2009, p. 76, p. 282). In the context of this research it does not make sense to discuss the pros and cons regarding the quantity theory of money. Therefor I leave it by the definitions and conclusions above.

3. The Quantitative Easing Program by the Fed since 2008

The main objective of this research is to investigate the measures of the Fed's reaction to the financial crisis that started in 2007. Here, the main focus is on its impact on inflation. In the following a short overview about the economic crisis will be provided to give an understanding of the quantitative easing programs that were initiated by the Fed. These programs and their impact on inflation will be analyzed afterwards. Possible exit strategies will also be considered, which is caused by the fact that the US Fed is currently starting its exit.

3.1. The Economic Crisis 2008

In the beginning of 2007 the conditions of the American housing market worsened, caused by an economic bubble that affected many parts of the United States housing market. The market environment was now highly influenced by subprime mortgage delinquencies and foreclosures which led to a devaluation of attendant securities. In April 2007 the first corporations filed under Chapter 11 bankruptcy protections. Standard & Poor's and Moody's Investor Services downgraded over 100 bonds backed by second-lien subprime mortgages. One month later Bear Stearns, one of the most widely read market intelligence on Wall Street, liquidated two hedge funds that invested in several of mortgage-backed securities. In September 2007 even mortgage lenders overseas were finally provided by liquidity. In the end of 2007 the pressures on the financial market intensified, reflected in diminished liquidity in interbank funding markets (Federal Reserve Bank of St. Louis, 2014). In spring and summer of 2008 more and more financial corporations in the U.S. filed under Chapter 11 bankruptcy protection or were taken into ownership of the state. At this time the first economic stimulus packages were launched (Economic Stimulus act of 2008, Public law 110 - 185). The cycle accelerated and intensified and Standard & Poor's downgraded further bond insurers. Finally, on the 15th of September 2008 Lehman brothers, the fourth-largest investment bank of the U.S. filed bankruptcy. It was the largest bankruptcy which was filed under Chapter 11 in the history of the United States. The summit of the entire story was now anywhere noticeable. The consumer price index (CPI), which is used as a measure of inflation, was on a monthly basis (November 2008 – October 2008) about minus 1.9%. This was the climax of the disaster at which the Fed finally was most active. At this time it was an economic crisis that affected the entire globe.

3.2. United States QE1, QE2, QE3

The crisis and its aftermath are great challenges for the Federal Reserve of the United States. In response to rapidly deteriorating economic and financial conditions, the Federal Open Market Committee (FOMC) pushed the federal funds rate in late 2008 in a corridor of 0 to 0.25 percent (Lowell R. Ricketts, 2011) and the primary credit rate to 0.50 percent. The federal funds rate is an interest rate at which a depository institution like a bank lends funds maintained at the Federal Reserve to another depository institution overnight. The primary credit rate is a short-term rate charged for the most financially secure financial institutions, or in other words it is the discount rate charged for primary credit. Caused by the worsened conditions of the crisis the Fed turned to nontraditional policies and started large-scale asset purchases in the hundreds of billions of dollars range. These purchases included mortgage-backed securities and Treasury securities. This action is commonly called "quantitative easing", QE (Lowell R. Ricketts, 2011, p. 1). Beside other important actions the Fed has done in response of the crisis, the aforementioned QE-program is the main subject of investigation of this research. Nevertheless a few actions should be mentioned. In the middle of 2008, the Fed changed the mortgage lending rules. Fed Chairman Ben Bernanke stated that the rules "[...] prohibit lenders from making higher-priced loans without due regard for consumers' ability to make the scheduled payments and require lenders to verify the income and assets on which they rely when making the credit decision [...]" (Bernanke, Ben S., 2008, Testimony). By open market operations, like purchase programs and other broad-based programs like dollar swap lines,

Primary Dealer Credit Facility (PDF) and assistance to individual institutions like Bear Stearns or AIG, the Fed sought to stabilize and improve conditions in financial markets to limit the damage to the broader economy (The Federal Reserve Bank of San Francisco, 2014). The next part provides an overview of the entire quantitative easing program from the Fed with timetable and its monetary dimensions.

QE1 begins: *Nov. 25, 2008 – March 31, 2010*

The Fed initiates purchases of $500 billion in mortgage-backed securities. Furthermore it announces purchases of up to $100 billion in debt obligations of mortgage giants Fannie Mae, Freddie Mac, Ginnie Mae and Federal Home Loan Banks. In March 2009, the Fed expands the mortgage buying program and announces it would purchase $750 billion more in mortgage-backed securities and it would invest another $100 billion in Fannie and Freddie debt and purchase up to $300 billion of longer-term Treasury securities over a period of six months.

End of QE1: *March 31, 2010*

The Fed ended its QE1 program by completing the purchase of $1.25 Trillion in mortgage-backed securities, $300 billion in Treasury bonds and $175 billion in federal agency debt (Da Costa, P., 2014; Kuttner, Kenneth N., 2010, pp. 407 - 430).

QE2 begins: *Nov. 3, 2010 – June 30, 2011*

In November of 2010, the Fed starts purchasing $600 billion of longer dated treasuries, at a rate of $75 billion per month (Da Costa, P., 2014).

End of QE2: *June 30, 2011*

After completing the purchase of the previously announced $600 billion in bonds, which conducted at an even pace, the mortgage rates in the U.S. have tumbled and reached record lows.

QE3 begins: *Sept. 13, 2012 – Dec. 18, 2013*

In September of 2012 the Fed starts a new round of quantitative easing by buying another $40 billion in mortgage-backed securities every month. The most important issue on this third round of quantitative easing is its open-ended commitment, which means that the purchase-program continues each month until the economy improves "substantially". The FOMC votes to expand its program further in the end of 2012 and adds $45 billion worth of longer-term Treasury securities. The time period during which the Fed will keep interest rates near zero was extended from the end of 2014 to mid-2015 (Da Costa, P., 2014).

QE tapered: *Dec. 18, 2013 until now*

In the end of 2013, the U.S. Fed begins reducing its asset purchases from $85 billion per month to $75 billion, then to $65 billion per month, but maintains the program as unemployment remains high and inflation low. Furthermore the central bank continues to keep the federal funds rate at zero to 0.25 percent, and expects to keep it there at least as long as: "The unemployment rate remains above 6.5 percent and inflation remains contained, or the inflation rate lags behind the committee's 2 percent goal if the unemployment rate dips beneath the 6.5 percent threshold." (Da Costa, P., 2014).

After the end of QE2 there was another program which was called Operation Twist. The content of this program was the purchase of $400 billion of bonds with maturities of 6 to 30 years and the selling of bonds with maturities less than 3 years. The purpose of this program was the extension of the average maturity of the Fed's own portfolio. The important difference between QE1, QE2 and QE3 was the attempt to do what quantitative easing tries to do, without expanding the Fed's balance sheet by printing more money (Board of Governors of the Federal Reserve System, 2013).

3.3. The Economic Impact of the Program

The economic impact of the entire quantitative easing program, which was initiated by the U.S. Fed, is enormous. A study from the U.S. Fed from 2012 found out that QE1 and QE2 reduced the yield on the 10-year Treasury bond by about 100 basis points. The consumer spending in the United States has been increasing continuously and reached $9,740 Billion in the first quarter of 2013 from $8.999 Billion in the last quarter of 2008. It furthermore has possibly supported the bull-run in stocks since early 2009 which caused an impressive spike in the S&P 500. There is a lot of evidence that without the entire QE-program, markets could be heading rapidly downwards (Rad, H., Ramakrishnan, A., 2013). Nevertheless there is some concern about its negative impact on economy in the near future, especially on inflation. The most important concern is about the enormous excess reserves which were generated through QE. The majority of economics and scientists are convinced that the absolute and the relative sizes of excess reserves are a big problem for the U.S. Fed as well as the general public because of their inflationary potential. But, like all contingencies, the scale and the timing of the detriment reserve-driven inflation might cause are uncertain. Todd (2013) notes that "It is even possible today to find articles in both scholarly circles and the popular press arguing either that the inflationary blow off might never happen or that an increasing tendency toward prolonged deflation is the more probable outcome." (Walker, F. Todd, 2013, p. 1).

Figure 1: M1 Money Multiplier, Source: St. Louis Fed Economic Data

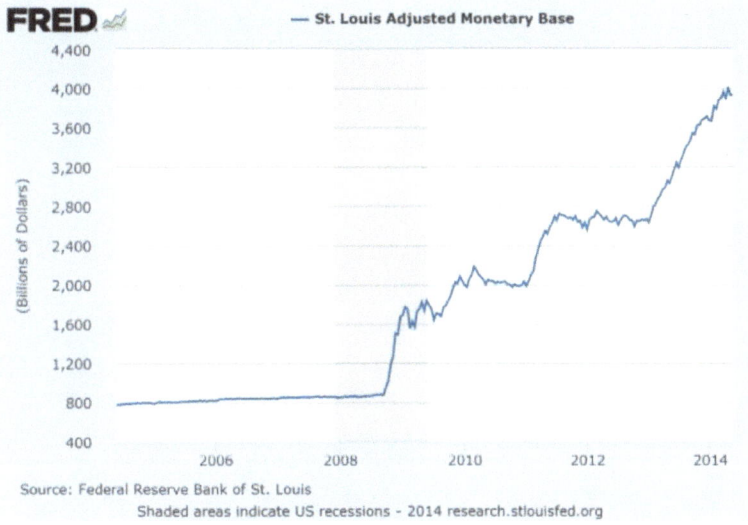

Figure 2: M1 The Monetary Base, Source: St. Louis Fed Economic Data

QE caused an enormous rise in the monetary base and a collapse of the money multiplier. The impact on both dimensions is almost proportional. This is reasoned by the incredible increase of so called excess reserves. These reserves are the excess or surplus of reserves against deposits and other liabilities that depository institutions (banks) hold above the amounts that are set by the central bank (Todd, F. Walker, 2013, p. 2). After the emergency lending activities in late 2008 the excess increased from less than $2 billion of excess reserves to $767 billion by year-end 2008. During the crisis in the 1930s excess reserves were also built up but this time with an important difference. For the first time in history of the U.S. the Fed pays interest on all reserves, required and excess reserves (Todd, F. Walker, 2013, p. 2).

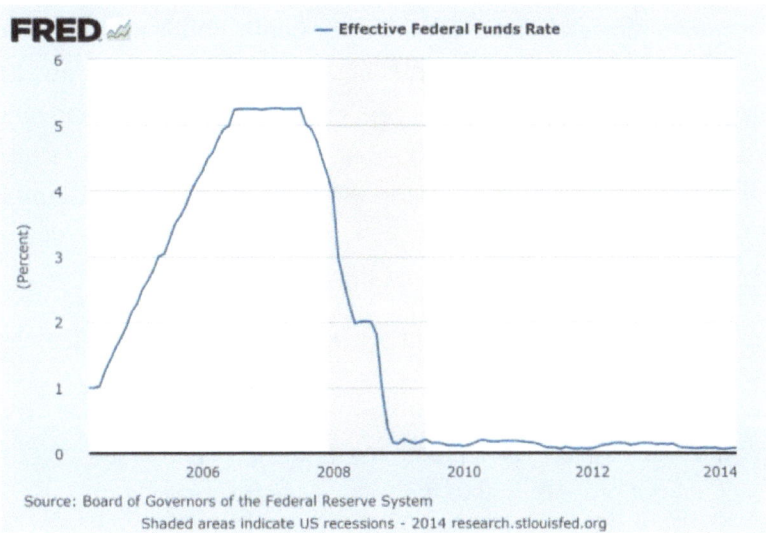

Figure 3: Federal Funds Rate, Source: St. Louis Fed Economic Data

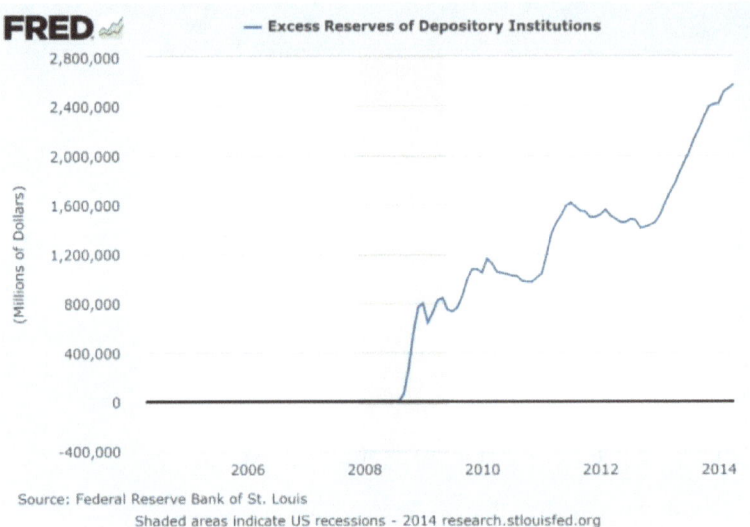

Figure 4: Excess Reserves, Source: St. Louis Fed Economic Data

In the following the correlation between the dimensions shown above is explained by the formulas introduced and described under part 2 of this research.

$$\Delta B = C + \Delta R \Rightarrow \uparrow B = C + \uparrow R$$

Following this equation, an increase in reserves will lead to an increase in the monetary base. But due to the interest which is paid for reserves, the multiplier process does not come into play. The interest the Fed pays and deems appropriate is below the maximum of the target band of the federal funds rate. At this point where the market interest rate is almost zero, banks no longer face an opportunity cost of holding reserves and the money multiplier effect is absent (Todd Keister, James J. McAndrews, 2009, p. 8). In fact the banks rather get paid for their excess reserves by the Fed than lending them out. The lack of the multiplier effect leads to an almost stable development of the money supply, illustrated in the following charts. This correlation can also be explained by using the dimensions from part 2 of this research.

$$M = m \cdot B = m \cdot (C + R) \Rightarrow \Delta M = \Delta m \cdot (C + \Delta R) \Rightarrow \uparrow M = \downarrow m \cdot (C + \uparrow \uparrow R)$$

If the increase of the amount of reserves is larger than the decrease of the money multiplier, money supply increases as well but not proportional to the increase of reserves.

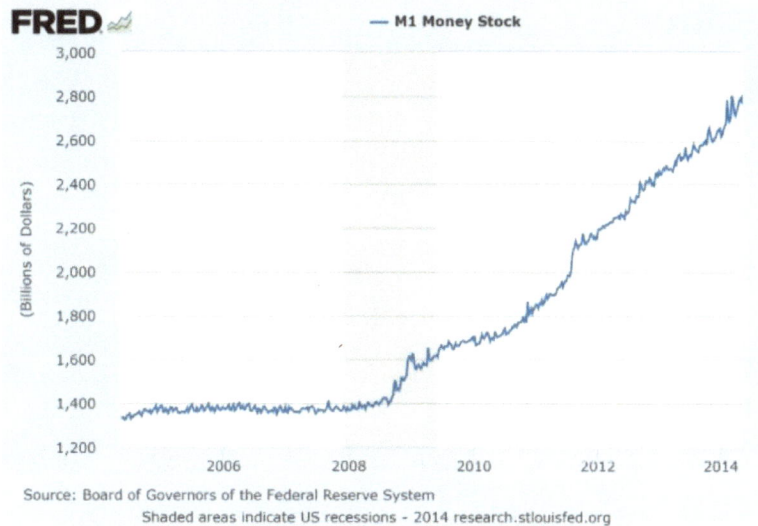

Figure 5: M1 Money Stock, Source: St. Louis Fed Economic Data

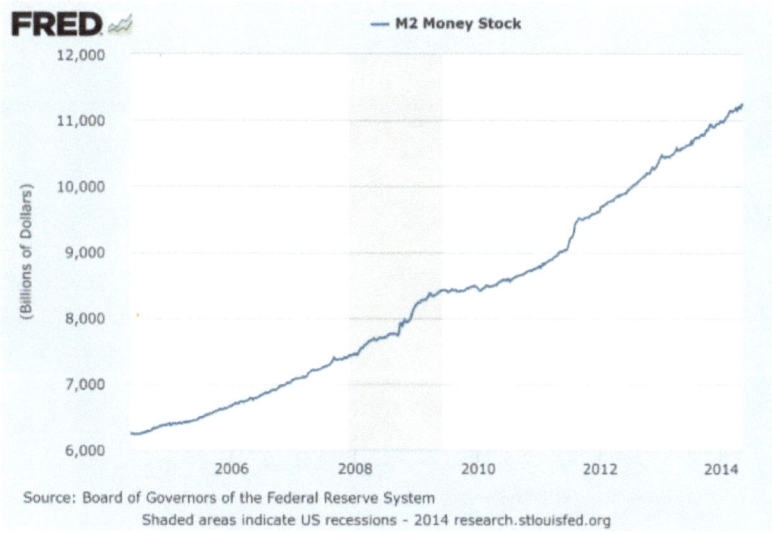

Figure 6: M2 Money Stock, Source: St. Louis Fed Economic Data

That the amount of currency as Federal Reserve Notes in circulation is stable and not changing over a large period of time you can be seen in Fig.9 (next side) in the chart of assets and Liabilities of the Federal Reserve. Using this assumption and evaluating the development of GDP and the M2 Money Stock we can easily conclude by the quantity theory of money that a change in the CPI of all items in the same time will never reach a magnitude like it appears in the monetary base or money multiplier which is shown in Fig. 1.

Figure 7: CPI of all Items, Source: St. Louis Fed Economic Data

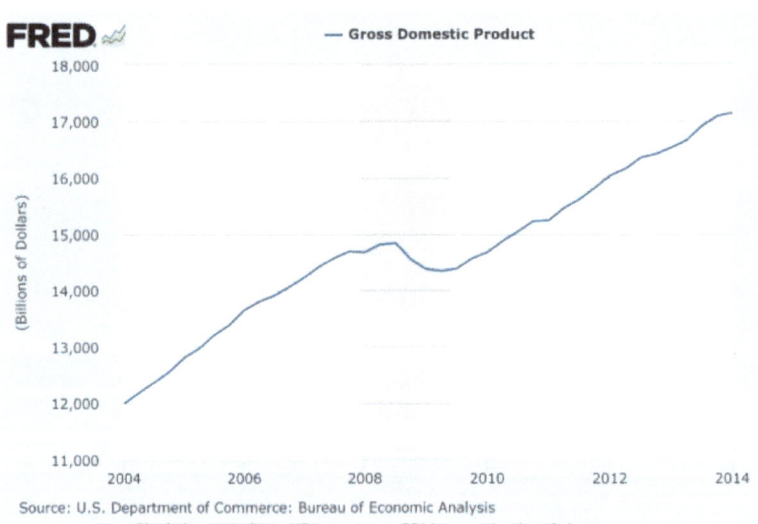

Figure 8: GDP, Source: St. Louis Fed Economic Data

$$\pi = \frac{\Delta M}{M} - \frac{\Delta Y}{Y} = \frac{\Delta P}{P}$$

Therefore we can conclude quantitatively that QE has no current effect or impact on inflation. The reason why the classical macroeconomic doctrine does not work as expected is reasoned by excess reserves which emerged as a by-product of the QE-program. It can be assumed that as long as the interest rate on (excess) reserves is higher than the upper band of the Fed Funds Rate, excess reserves remain more attractive "[..] than selling them as Fed funds because they can be rolled over at no cost and can be liquidated without waiting for a day to pass" (Dwyer, Gerald P., 2009). Todd (2013) notes aptly that "There is no obvious reason why excess reserves will decline as long as they are similar to risk-free assets.".

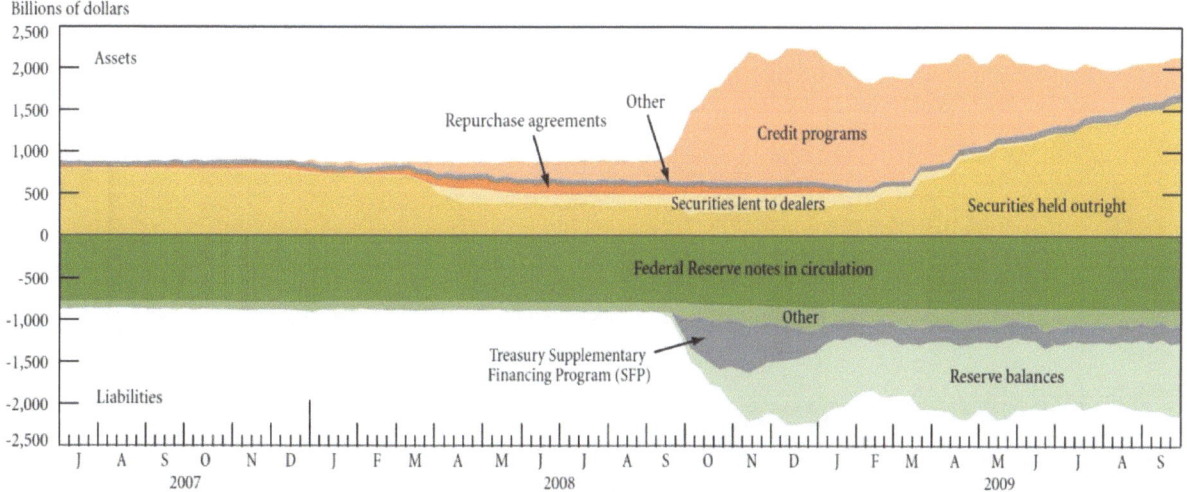

Figure 9: Assets and Liabilities of the Federal System of the U.S., Source: Federal Reserve Statistical Release H.4.1

As long as excess reserves are not used in the traditional way and banks holding excess reserves will not seek to lend out those reserves at any positive interest rate, money creation will not exist as it is thought, inflation neither. But if the multiplier process is able to work again, additional lending creates additional deposits in the banking system and the process then repeats itself, with banks making more new loans and the short-term interest rate falling further. So the main risk is losing control of the excess reserves by the Fed or different spoken an increasing economic revival that leads to money creation by demand of cash from the public and net payments to the private sector. Nevertheless it should be mentioned, that a large part of economists, scientists and analysts have the opinion that banks are not able to use excess reserves for making loans. The most popular article is from Paul Sheard, Global Chief Economist and Head of Global Economics and Research at Standard and Poor's, New York, from August 2013 in which he claims that banks are technically not capable to use excess reserves for making loans. He says: "Many talk as if banks can "lend out" their reserves, raising concerns that massive excess reserves created by QE could fuel runaway credit creation and inflation in the future. But banks cannot lend their reserves directly to commercial borrowers, so this concern is misplaced." (Sheard, P., 2013, p. 2). But it is not really clear why they should not be able to use excess reserves for other investments than as deposits at the Fed. Because they are excess reserves and not required reserves so they are not constrained to hold these reserves. However I agree that an alternative use of excess reserves must be initiated by demand from outside the banking sector, or rather the public. Because in fiat credit-based economies, lending comes first, reserves come second.

3.4. The Exit Strategy

What often is neglected is that the issue with excess reserves is not new. There is even a recent example of how excess reserves could be reduced without harming the economy or open the Pandora's Box of inflation. Between 2004 and 2005, as the economy recovered from the severe crisis around the turn of the millennium (Dot-com bubble), Japan attempted just such an exit (Yamaoka, H., Syed, M., 2010, p. 1 - 10). Without going into details, a short impression should be given about the dimensions and the context by the following chart that express the extent of Quantitative Easing in Japan between 2001 and 2007.

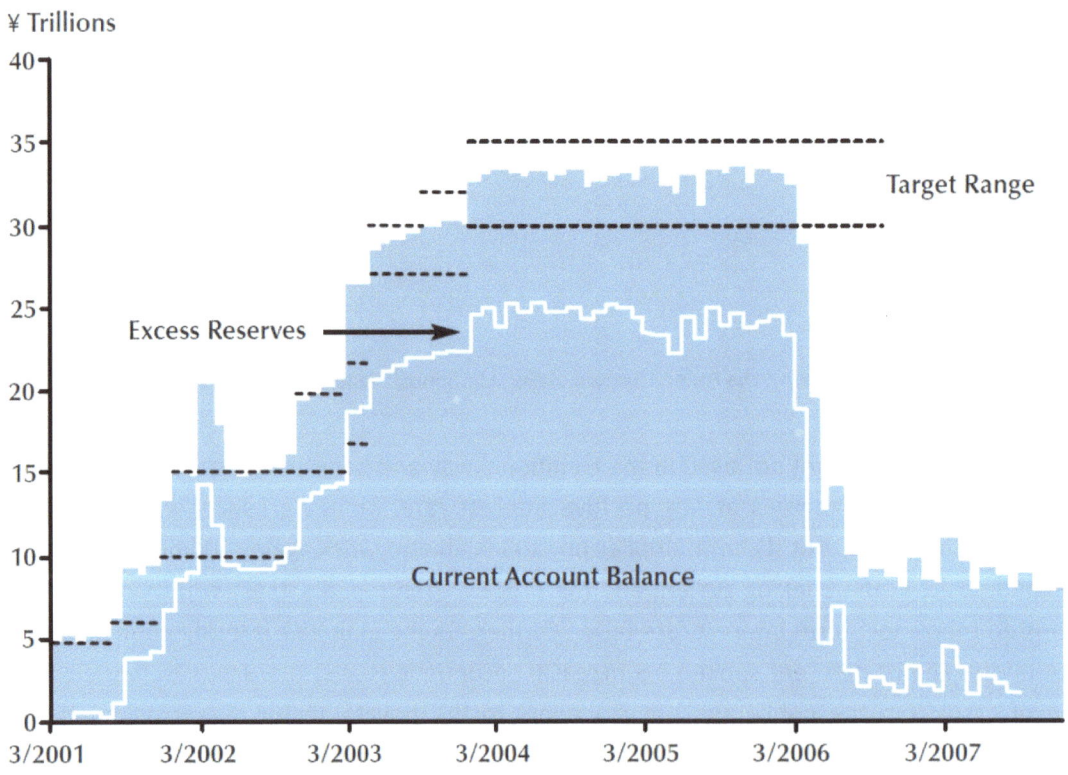

Figure 10: Quantitative Easing in Japan, Source: Bank of Japan

It might be concluded that the abrupt withdrawal of central bank money was driven by fears of incipient inflation. Or it maybe was the reason why inflation never showed up (Blinder, Alan S., 2010, p. 465 - 479). Therefore some lessons learned should be considered by the Fed, although the conditions and the content of the program in Japan are a bit different from the recent situation.

By July 2006 the Bank of Japan (BoJ) had downsized its balance sheet before raising the policy rate. "Clear communication, transparent conditions governing future actions, flexibility, and market confidence about the adequacy of tools and underlying strategy for absorbing excess liquidity helped the BoJ manage an orderly exit." (Yamaoka, H., Syed, M., 2010, p. 6).

In order to repurchase excess reserves, the Fed can sell securities, such as government bonds, to the commercial banks. This is challenging because of its potential market impact and potential central bank losses. The BoJ, for example, purchased assets with short maturities (ABCP) and those with longer maturities (JGB and stocks). If risk appetite recovers, the former could simply be held to maturity, while assets with longer maturities needed a strategy of selling to minimize potential negative impacts on markets. In the current context, the composition of the assets that the Fed has acquired will in large part determine their approach to exit (Yamaoka, H., Syed, M., 2010, p. 13). To exit from unconventional easing a number of seemingly straightforward central bank operations are involved to maintain activity close to potential and ensure price stability (Yamaoka, H., Syed, M., 2010, p. 6):

- Halting extraordinary interventions
- Downsizing and normalizing the central bank balance sheet
- Selling purchased assets (if necessary)
- Raising short-term interest rates

Overall the exit from QE in Japan has been considered a success (Van Rixtel, A., 2009, Executive summary). As the BoJ announced its exit in March 2006 it reduced rapidly the most flexible assets on their balance sheet which was the amount of its bills purchases from private banks, to match the rapid decline in the amount of excess reserves. The balance sheet adjustments were conducted through operations directly with the banking sector, which facilitated the management of the exit process. The BoJ reduced its holdings of Japanese government securities very slowly and moderately in order not to distort supply and demand conditions in bond markets. The gradual reduction of securities was mainly realized by reducing the amount of short-term government securities. The crucial result the Japanese experience shows is that activity in interbank markets becomes very subdued (Van Rixtel, A., 2009, Executive summary).

4. Conclusion

What we are able to conclude securely is that there is no current impact of QE from the Fed on inflation. However the liquidity facilities and other credit programs introduced by the Federal Reserve in response to the crisis have created, as a by-product, a large quantity of reserves in the banking system (Todd Keister, James J. McAndrews, 2009, pp. 1 - 8). Nevertheless this dramatic buildup of excess reserves conveys no information about the effects of these initiatives on bank lending or on the level of economic activity. The largest concern about the end of QE is how to reduce excess reserves appropriately. What we learned is that the common macroeconomic doctrine as it is thought is obsolete because of the environment of interest which is paid on excess reserves. Nevertheless if banks are able and willing to use their excess reserves for lending, the multiplier effect comes into play again. If this will happen the chance is great to experience new dimensions of inflation. So the main topic for the Fed will be the reduction of excess reserves. During the Great Depression between 1930 and 1940 the Fed had also built up excess reserves which were about 55 percent of the total reserves. Banks' lending for government guaranteed defense production programs gradually eroded the quantity of excess reserves (Todd, F. Walker, 2013, p. 11). Hopefully we will not see strategies like this neither in the near nor in the far future. So how can the Fed find strategies to manage an orderly exit from QE? We have seen that the Bank of Japan had already experienced exit procedures. The Fed can learn from this experience by using mechanism that Japan used, even if the current situation is a bit different. The composition of the assets that the Fed has acquired will in large part determine their approach to exit. If inflationary pressures begin to appear and the crisis-related programs are still in place, the central bank can also use its interest-on-reserves policy to raise interest rates without necessarily removing all of the newly created reserves (Todd Keister, James J. McAndrews, 2009, pp. 1 - 8). Last but not least I would give for thought that the concern about potential inflation in correlation with excess reserves maybe is misplaced. The chart in the following shows rather a correlation between a growing confidence in an economic recovering and QE conducted by the Fed. A poorly managed exit from QE may lead to a new economic uncertainty, but to that further investigation is necessary.

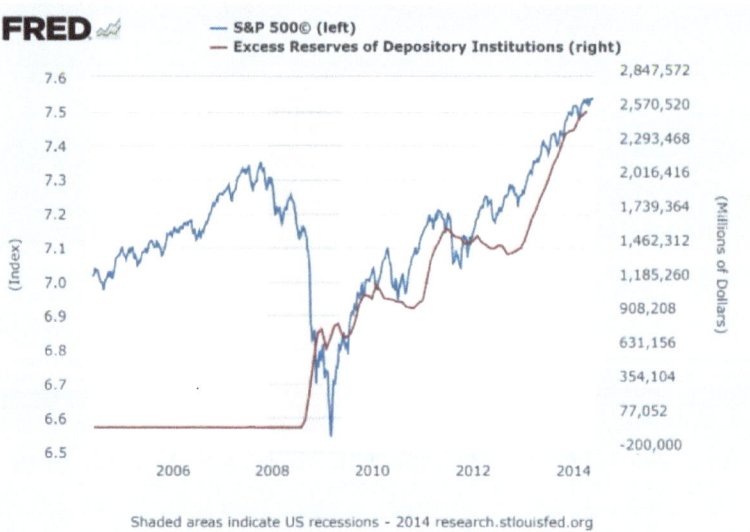

Figure 11: The S&P 500 compared with the amount of excess reserves, Source: St. Louis Fed Economic Data

Figure 12: The S&P 500 compared with U.S. Treasury securities held by the Fed, Source: St. Louis Fed Economic Data

Bibliography

Books

Amy, W. Grady (2011): *Macroeconomics: Developed Into an Exact Science*, 2nd edn., Raleigh, North Carolina: Lulu.

Ball, R. James (2009): *Inflation and the Theory of Money*, 2nd edn., Chicago: Aldine Pub. Co.

Jain, T.R., Khanna, O.P., Grover, M.L., Jain, D.K. (2006): *Macroeconomics*, 6th edn., New Delhi: V.K. Publications.

Michl, Thomas R. (2002): *Macroeconomic Theory: A Short Course*, first edn., Armonk, Ney York: M.E. Sharpe, Inc.

Friedman, M. (2009): The Optimum Quantity Of Money, 4th edn., New Brunswick, New Jersey: Transaction Publishers.

Papers, Lectures

Blinder, Alan S. (2010): Quantitative Easing: Entrance and Exit Strategies, *Federal Reserve Bank of St. Louis Review*, vol. 92, no. 6, pp. 465 - 479.

Kuttner, Kenneth N. (2010): The Fed's response to the financial crisis: Pages from the BOJ playbook, or a whole new ball game? *Public Policy Review*, Policy Research Institute, Ministry of Finance, Japan, vol. 6, no. 3, pp. 407-430.

Lowell R. Ricketts (2011): Quantitative Easing Explained, *Economic Information Newsletter*, Research Library of the Federal Reserve Bank of St. Louis, April 2011.

Mankiw, N. Gregory (2013): *The Monetary System: What It Is and How It Works* [Lecture to Macroeconomics Analyses], *ECO 62: Instructor: Udayan, R.* Long Island University. 21 February 2014.

Sheard, P. (2013): *Repeat After Me: Banks Cannot And Do Not "Lend Out" Reserves*, Economic Research, August 13, 2013, Standard & Poor's Ratings Services, New York.

Todd, F. Walker (2013): The Problem of Excess Reserves, Then and Now, *Levy Economics Institute of Bard College Working Paper*, no. 763, May 2013.

Todd Keister, James J. McAndrews, (2009): Why Are Banks Holding So Many Excess Reserves?, *Federal Reserve Bank of New York current issues IN ECONOMICS AND FINANCE*,
vol. 15, no. 8, pp. 1-8.

Van Rixtel, A., (2009): *The exit from Quantitative Easing (QE): The Japanese experience*, International Financial Markets Division, Associate Directorate General International Affairs, Bank of Spain.

Yamaoka, H., Syed, M., (2010): *Managing the Exit: Lessons from Japan's Reversal of Unconventional Monetary Policy*, IMF Working Paper, International Monetary Fund, vol. 10, no. 114, pp. 1-14.

Reports

Da Costa, P. (2014): *Financial crisis timeline: Collapse and bailout*. Available at: http://www.bankrate.com [Accessed 12 May 2014].

Dwyer, Gerald P. (2009): *Interest on Reserves and the Current High Level of Excess Reserves*, Federal Reserve Bank of Atlanta, Available at http://www.frbatlanta.org [Accessed 12 May 2014].

Federal Reserve Bank of St. Louis, Research Division (2014): *Monetary Trends*. St. Louis. Available at: http://research.stlouisfed.org/ [Accessed 12 May 2014].

U.S. Department of Labor (2008): *CPI Detailed Report, Data for November 2008*. Washington: Bureau of Labor Statistics. Available at: http://www.bls.gov/cpi [Accessed 11 May 2014].

Websites

Bernanke, Ben S. (2008): *Financial Markets, the Economic Outlook, and Monetary Policy*. Available at: http://www.federalreserve.gov [Accessed 11 May 2014].

Bernanke, Ben S. (2008): Testimony, Semiannual Monetary Policy Report to the Congress. Available at: http://federalreserve.gov [Accessed 12 May 2014].

Board of Governors of the Federal Reserve System (2013): *Maturity Extension Program and Reinvestment Policy*. Available at: http://www.federalreserve.gov [Accessed 12 May 2014].

Doom, P. (2012): *Markets Await 'Helicopter Ben,' But May Be Disappointed*. Available at: http://www.cnbc.com [Accessed 11 May 2014].

Federal Reserve Bank of St. Louis (2014): *The Financial Crisis – A Timeline of Events and Policy Actions.* Available at: http://timeline.stlouisfed.org [Accessed 11 May 2014].

Rad, H., Ramakrishnan, A. (2013): Impact of Quantitative Easing on business: What do we need to know? Available at: http://mu-sigma.com [Accessed 12 May 2014].

The Federal Reserve Bank of San Francisco (2014): *Fed's Response*. Available at: http://sffed-education.org [Accessed 12 May 2014].